CELEBRATING
IDENTITY

CELEBRATING IDENTITY

A RESOURCE MANUAL

for practitioners working with Black children and young people including Black children of mixed parentage

compiled by

Christine Chambers

Sue Funge

Gail Harris and

Cynthia Williams

Trentham Books

First published in 1996 by Trentham Books Limited

Trentham Books Limited
Westview House
734 London Road
Oakhill
Stoke-on-Trent
Staffordshire
England ST4 5NP

British Cataloguing in Publication Data
A catalogue record for this book is available from the British Library
ISBN: 1 85856 068 3

Cover: we thank the Birmingham Development Education
Centre for permission to use the photograph from *Behind the Scenes*.

Designed and typeset by Trentham Print Design Ltd., Chester
and printed in Great Britain by The Book Factory, London.

Yowie, yowie, my brown skin baby
They take him away.
Between her sobs I heard her say
Police 'bin take my baby away,
From white man boss baby I had,
Why he let them take baby away?

To a children's home the baby came
With new clothes on and a new name,
But day and night he would always say,
Mummy, oh mummy why they take me away?
Yowie, yowie, my brown skin baby
They take him away.

Bob Randall

Children could be taken away from their Aboriginal mothers, especially those who had a white father. They were put in special children's homes and brought up away from their families. It was to try to make the Aboriginal people lose their culture, that is, to give up their way of life and become like white Australians. This is part of a song written by one of these children when he grew up and became a singer and songwriter.

World Studies 8-13 Making Global Connections:
A World Studies Workbook
edited by David Hicks
and Miriam Steiner, 1989, p.65.

ACKNOWLEDGMENTS

We thank our wonderful children for being who they are and for the part they have played in inspiring us in our work. The contribution from the parents and children of Oxford's Black Child Mixed Parentage Group is greatly appreciated. We also wish to thank Oxfordshire County Council Social Services Department for their support in the compilation of this resource manual. Special thanks to Anne Peake for her contribution regarding a white perspective on the developmental stages that may be worked through to achieve anti-racist practice. To Gill Howe for the model of experiences of oppression and discrimination and to Parveen Sheikh and Lena Lai, social work students who contributed to our discussions.

The Early Years Trainers Anti-Racist Network (EYTARN) provided useful guidance through their publications and conferences. Special thanks also to Sue Lewis and Paul Holland for their invaluable help with the manuscript.

We hope we have acknowledged all relevant publishers regarding the sources of some of the information included in this resource but if we have failed to contact anyone please accept our apology; it is not our intention to forget anyone.

CONTENTS

THE AUTHORS

Christine Chambers – When my father arrived in England from Ireland in 1959, much prejudice still existed here towards the Irish. But his children were white so we were absorbed into, and accepted by, society. My children's paternal grandparents arrived here from Jamaica at around the same time. Irish and Jamaican were both English-speaking, each with their own cultures and history. The difference was that their Jamaican grandparents were Black. I can talk openly, if I choose to, of my Irish roots and this is tolerated, even indulged. The issue for me is that I can choose whether to reveal my ancestry. My Black children do not have the same choice. My children have much to offer society and I hope they will never have to compromise their pride in being Black so as to be allowed to do so.

I see this resource manual as indicative of a future for *all* children in this society. I firmly believe that society has been enriched by becoming multiracial. I am often embarrassed by my ignorance about other people's history, culture or religion but I am eager to learn and not too proud to ask. I believe we should be ashamed of our ignorance only if we lose the desire to learn.

Sue Funge – I am very pleased to be involved in the production of this resource. I am a white mother with a Black son aged twelve and feel very strongly about the need to challenge racism effectively. It can be a very difficult, painful and sensitive issue to address but it is necessary if we are to build a better future for all our children. It can be uncomfortable as a white person to acknowledge racism – to acknowledge that a lot of the information we have received through-out our lives, particularly in our early years and education, has hidden the contribution of Black people and boasted the superiority of the white European. It continues to be a learning process but the first stage is to be willing to overcome the awkwardness of not knowing about Black history, cultures, achievements etc. Once I had acknowledged my own ignorance I was able to begin to find out. It continues to be an enlightening experience and at times makes me feel outraged that I never knew about so many wonderful things. For example, as a child I would sometimes ask my dad where he was going, and he would reply Timbuktu. I always believed it was an imaginary place, a bit of a joke. Imagine my surprise when I learnt that in fact it was the home of the first university!

Gail Harris – As a parent and social worker, initially working with families with young children and for the last eight years with childcare providers, I have become increasingly aware of the importance of creating caring environments, where the needs of all children are taken into account.

Watching my daughters growing up I can appreciate how, for each child to achieve their full potential, their individual needs have to be recognised and addressed. The Children Act, with its emphasis on the welfare of the child and taking into account children's needs arising from race, culture, religion and language, has provided for me a backdrop to this manual. I hope this resource will enhance our understanding and support of the children of mixed parentage and their families with whom we come into contact so that their individual needs can be addressed in a sensitive and appropriate manner.

Cynthia Williams – As a Black child of the 1950s growing up in a predominantly white rural environment I experienced racism at school and in the community. I was not aware then of the consequences of prejudice and racism and its potential effect on all children, Black and white. From that early childhood experience there are two key values that I hold to be important. One is that Black children should not be brought up in racial isolation and the other is that they must be cared for in an environment where they are helped to cope with the racism they may encounter throughout their lives. This greatly influenced my decision as a parent to bring up my daughter in a multicultural community, where she would value not only herself but others from different cultural backgrounds.

Throughout my professional life as a social worker, I have tried to raise an awareness amongst my colleagues of the importance of nurturing a positive Black identity for Black and mixed parentage children and young people. Being a part of the team who compiled this resource manual has enabled me to further this work. I hope that it will provide a balance of theory and practical guidance and raise the profile of work against racism within the childcare setting. It is only through an openness and willingness to learn from each other and with each other that we will move this work forward. It has been most rewarding to work with the parents of the Oxford Black Child Mixed Parentage support group and my colleagues in Social Services.

FOREWORD

(taken from the keynote address at the launch of the pilot for this resource manual, on May 14 1996)

I believe that this publication is an extremely valuable contribution to a growing and much needed body of knowledge and if material such as this had been available when I was growing up that my own life chances would have been greatly enhanced.

The manual is an outstanding illustration of how professional values *and* ethics and good practice emerge out of personal experience and a dogged determination to fight oppression and improve the human condition. After reading and reflection I decided to approach the task of launching it in the spirit of the whole initiative: that is, to join in the celebration of identity.

Today I can celebrate the fact that inter-racial marriages and inter-personal relationships are a common feature of our culture (there is lots of 'black in the union jack'), and I also celebrate the language or discourse of anti-racism, that enables us to tell it like it is and to assert the value of our being.

This resource pack, too, explores a range of responses that most of us are familiar with. For black children and children of mixed parentage these include: *rejection, bewilderment, frustration, lack of positive self-esteem, feelings of shame concerning skin colour, hair, language.* For white children racism tends to: *foster a sense of superiority, distort concepts of fairness and equality, and perpetuate oppression.*

I agree entirely with the authors and admire their diligence in detailing the dynamics of identity formation and how racism is experienced in early childhood. They explain clearly not only what racism does, but the processes through which it operates and shapes personal and social identity. The focus that they place on the needs of the growing child reminded me poignantly that as a young child, I had no understanding of 'racism' – in fact the term as we know it was not yet formulated.

During the last few days I have attempted to put recent developments in our understanding of racism into perspective and re-evaluate what they mean for me personally. This has entailed getting back in touch with two configurations of feelings: first, in my early childhood pain, fear, shock and confusion; and as I grew older frustration, anger and indignation. Put another way, my understanding of pain, fear and shock/confusion has come through my experience of racism; and my black identity has emerged out of my resistance to the injustices that many of us have experienced and or witnessed.

My pain and fear was of being verbally and physically abused, ridiculed, rejected, despised and excluded. Racist taunts in the playground, threats from bullies, racist attacks were part of my childhood experience. The shock and confusion brought on by such incidents had several dimensions. The very fact that I was the focus of such aggression, in many instances out of the blue, was in itself painful. But along with this came the realisation that I was vulnerable (ie black) and that I would not change the condition that made me vulnerable.

For an 'isolated' child this is a confusing situation. By isolated I mean a child that does not have the support to develop a secure black identity. The isolated child often does not know what is happening, and comes to accept the aggressors' explanations because there is no one to explain why they are the victims of such outrages. This confusion is deepened when the outrage stems from a parent or a trusted adult. For this constitutes a betrayal by the very person or people that a black child or a child of mixed parentage turns to first

for support. The shock of betrayal reinforces the pain of rejection and undermines *all* sense of belonging. Fortunately, I did not experience this ultimate betrayal, but I was isolated in an educational system that did not acknowledge or perhaps understand what was happening.

I shall share one example with you. It happened in secondary school when I was 12. For one period each week every member of the class was required to read – aloud a paragraph from a set novel. This was my introduction to the work of Mark Twain: *The Adventures of Huckleberry Finn* a popular American story of the adventures of two young country boys and their adult companion and mentor, Jim. Now Jim is a black man: more precisely, in Mark Twain's terms, a 'nigger'. In the narrative he is variously and frequently described as 'Jim the nigger', 'nigger Jim' or just plain 'nigger'. Dear old Jim featured prominently in Huck and Tom's adventures and there is scarcely a paragraph in the whole book in which the word nigger does not occur. But there are a few. I know this to be so because those were the ones that I read to the class. I suppose I have to thank the sensitivity of my English teacher for this concession. He must have had some understanding that the only 'coloured' boy in the class might feel uncomfortable reading out the word 'nigger'. This concern however must not be seen as the beginnings of an effective anti-racist education strategy in Friern Barnet Secondary Modern School. For I have a clear memory of being in that class with my eyes focused rigidly on the page, overwhelmed by abject stultifying paralysis. It may not surprise you to know that I failed 'O' level English literature.

Nowadays this would be acknowledged for what it was – racial abuse – and that is a welcome development. There is less chance of a black child being exposed to such overt racism today. But I cannot feel complacent – when in 1991, I outlined this experience to a group of teachers. I was surprised at their vigorous defence of the book and their willingness to use it in class. This episode, among others, reinforced my conviction that we as parents and members of the black community must be ever vigilant of the quality of the education our children receive. We cannot assume that all professionals have the insight and understanding to provide appropriate learning material for a multi-racial society. But my comments may be seen as unwelcome political correctness, that has already claimed dear old Noddy and all those harmless golliwogs.

Surviving experiences of racism during my early childhood has served me well later as a social worker – and in this I am not unique. Most black social workers can intuitively convey a warm empathy to black children and develop an almost immediate unspoken trust and rapport. It is born out of a shared experience of oppression. I do not wish to imply that only black social workers (and allied professionals) have this potential. But as a social work educator I am very aware of the many anxieties that white professionals and students experience when attempting to meet the needs of black children and children of mixed parentage. This resource manual will play a valuable role in building confidence and competence because it addresses, in very accessible terms, key areas of identity development that many texts tend to ignore or mystify. And this knowledge and understanding is vital for the development of competent social workers, be they white or black – because competent practice demands more than intuition. Therefore, I celebrate a resource that is going to both enhance my competence as a teacher and promote the development of more effective anti-racist practice.

Moving on the importance of a black identity, my experiences of frustration, anger and indignation have been the driving force of the development of my black identity, which took place during the 1960s against the backdrop of Martin Luther King's movement for civil rights and the Black Panthers' assertion of Black Power. These movements were highly significant in focusing and crystallising the resistance to racism and asserting a sense of belonging and identity

emerging out of a new black consciousness: 'I am black and I am proud'. These movements are an essential aspect of the black heritage. And even though the rhetoric may sound a little archaic the same key issue underlies today's concerns – that is, power.

The power to define who you are? The power to insist that every child has equal opportunity? The power to overcome marginalisation, alienation and frustration? Nowadays such power is emerging out of, among other things, the growing number of constructive inter-racial relationships; out of the celebration of identity; out of the networks established between various organisations; out of the commitment of informed professionals working in partnership with parents and children. They will enhance the development of a constructive racial identity of all people, black and white, in our country. Our identity is forged out of our resistance to oppression and our assertion of belonging. Without it, all strategies to cope with the fear, pain and confusion that are unavoidable aspects of the black experience, are futile.

Of late I have heard much criticism of the lack of specificity about the duty to pay 'due consideration' to racial, cultural and linguistic factors enshrined in the 1989 Children Act. Surely the critical issue is lack of understanding of the significance of these factors rather than of the meaning of 'due consideration'. This resource manual brings much needed clarity. It is refreshing and stimulating blend of theoretical perspectives and practical techniques that integrates *antiracist* and *ethnically sensitive* knowledge and skills and presents them in a coherent and accessible manner.

It incorporates an understanding of the nature and history of racism and its effects upon social institutions and individual attitudes and expectations; a detailed and informed evaluation of key perspectives upon personal and racial identity formation; and, most importantly, an emphasis upon a child's need to define her or his own identity. It highlights that identity is not fixed and static and that we are not inevitably doomed to be victims of an oppressive racist society – we have the power and techniques to change things.

In my experience, not many texts achieve this: racism is too often depicted as a pervasive omnipotent force, with little explanation of how it operates other than, in Phil Cohen's words 'it's racism wot dun it'. This resource pack:

- acknowledges the widespread and damaging effects of racism

- explains how these effects occur

- offers exercises to redress these effects and

- provides details of a supportive network.

I am not suggesting that this achievement is unique – other than the choice of keynote speaker at the launch! However, Chambers *et al* 1996 have produced a resource manual that provides caring professionals with the knowledge and tools to develop an empowering therapeutic strategy.

Ray Coker
Lecturer in Social Work, Southampton Institute

PART ONE
Being young and Black in Britain

People working with young children should value and respect the different racial origins, religions, cultures and languages in a multiracial society so that each child is valued as an individual without racial or gender stereotyping. Children from a very young age learn about different races and cultures including religion and languages and will be capable of assigning different values to them. ... It is important that people working with young children are aware of this so that their practice enables the children to develop positive attitudes to differences of race, culture and language and differences of gender. ... Children should have the right to be cared for as part of a community which values the religious, racial, cultural and linguistic identity of the child. The justification for the awarding of such a right would be in terms of fostering the child's sense of identity. Children's sense of identity is a fundamental aspect of their development. (Statements in the Children Act 1989 Guidance notes as cited in *Children without Prejudice* BBC Educational Developments, 1994)

This manual aims to provide a useful tool for all those working with children and young people who wish to address the potentially negative effects of racism on nurturing positive self identity. Acknowledging the existence of racism can be difficult for people who believe that they treat all children the same. However, as Naomi Eisenstadt observes:

We can no longer tolerate the oft-heard comment with respect to (discrimination): 'We don't discriminate, we treat everyone the same'. We now know that 'treating everyone the same' is discriminatory in that it fails to account for differences within and between groups. (*Selecting for Equality*, EYTARN, 1995)

Working together on this manual, we have been able to share the perspectives of being Black and growing up in Britain, and of being white bringing up Black children in Britain. In our experience there appears to be little distinction drawn between Black children with two Black parents and Black children of mixed parentage, when they are outside the home environment.

> When my son walks into a shop he is followed around the store just as any Black boy of a similar age is followed. I don't believe that any security staff in a store are thinking 'Ah, now he is half-white so I don't need to check him out'. The stereotype image of young Black males affects my child as much as any other Black child. I strongly believe we need to acknowledge that racism exists and that we, as white people, should stop feeling afraid to admit we are racist. How can we move on and provide a better world for our children if we don't look to our own part in creating that world? (White mother with a Black child)

A Black child or young person of mixed parentage may try and deny their Black heritage as they come to realise that being Black is portrayed as being inferior to white. Challenging this portrayal will benefit not only Black children but all children, as they begin to discover the positive contribution Black people have made throughout history and continue to make today. Black people have had to cope with a society that often accords them little or no respect. A Black child nurtured in an environment where there is an awareness of the effect this may have is more likely to find the strength to resist these negative messages than a child who is cared for by people who hope that ignoring the issue will prevent it affecting the child.

This manual is designed to help those wishing to learn more about the implications of racism and how we can work towards providing an anti-racist environment that will benefit all children. We believe that if we wish to celebrate *all* children, we must work to provide an environment in which every child and young person is valued and respected.

CHAPTER ONE

PUTTING RACISM INTO A HISTORICAL CONTEXT

To acquire an understanding about how entrenched racist attitudes have been perpetuated over the centuries it can be useful to look back to where some of these attitudes originate. As a result of racial prejudice Black children and young people and their families are often perceived as a 'problem' in our society. This can undermine their ability to develop a positive sense of identity.

In 1766, David Hume, who held a stewardship in a colonial office, remarked that:

> I am apt to suspect the negroes and in general all the other species of men (for there are four or five different kinds) to be naturally inferior to the whites. There never was a civilised nation of any other complexion than white, nor even any individual eminent either in action or speculation.

In 1772 Edward Long described miscegenation ('the interbreeding of races, especially of Whites and non-Whites') as:

> a venomous and dangerous ulcer that threatens to disperse its malignancy far and wide until every family catches infection from it ... The English blood will become so contaminated with this mixture ... till the whole nation resembles the Portuguese and Moriscos in complexion of skin and baseness of mind.

Charles Darwin, in *The Descent of Man* (1871) stated that:

> The races differ also in constitution, in acclimatisation, and in liability to certain diseases. Their mental characteristics are likewise very distinct; chiefly as it would appear in their emotional, but partly in their intellectual faculties. Everyone who has had the opportunity of comparison, must have been struck with the contrast between the taciturn, even morose, aborigines of South America and the light-hearted, talkative negroes.

In the twentieth century similar assertions continued to be made about the inferiority of people who are not white:

> The racial stocks most prolific of gifted children are those from northern and western Europe, and the Jewish. The least prolific are the Mediterranean races, the Mexicans and the Negroes. (Louis Terman, 1923)

> The half-caste appears in a prodigal literature. It presents him, to be frank, mostly as an undersized, scheming and entirely degenerate bastard. His father is a blackguard, his mother a whore. But more than all this, he is a potential menace to Western Civilisation, to everything that is White and Sacred and majusculed. (Cedric Dover, 1937)

In the magazine, *Glamour*, a question on the problem page in 1955 was answered thus:

> Many coloured men are fine people, but they do come from a different race with a very different background and upbringing. Besides, scientists do not yet know if it is wise for two such very different races as white and black to intermarry, for sometimes the children of mixed marriages seem to inherit the worst characteristics of each race.

Henry Garrett, in *Breeding Down* (1966), writes:

> You can no more mix the two races and maintain the standards of white civilisation than you can add 80 (the average IQ of Negroes) and 100 (the average IQ of whites), divide by two and get 100. What you would get would be a race of 90s, and it is that 10 per cent differential that spells the difference between a spire and a mud hut; 10 per cent – or less – is the margin between civilisation's 'profit'; it is the difference between a cultured society and savagery.

Over the span of two hundred years there has been little change in these attitudes for many people. There is still an underlying belief that white Europeans are the superior race and a general fear of what mixing the 'races' may mean for the future. However, these fears have no scientific basis. Biologically there is no significant difference between any of the so-called 'races':

> In practice, 'racial' categories are established that correspond to major skin colour groups, and all the border-line cases are distributed among these or are made into new races according to the whim of the scientist ... Human 'racial' differentiation is, indeed, only skin-deep. Any use of racial categories must take its justification from some other source than biology. (Rose, Lewontin and Kamin, *Not in Our Genes* 1981)

It is important to recognise that the views expressed in the quotes above continue to play their part in the formation of people's opinions today. If we are to help dispel these misinformed opinions we must be aware of the starting point. Mixed 'race' children would seem to strike at the very heart of a racist system; they threaten its existence by calling into question the categories upon which it is based. As Susan Benson (1981) says:

> To study the everyday life of interacial families ... is to study the nature of British race relations.

The effect on Black children and young people, whether of mixed 'race' parentage or not, can be to undermine their feelings of self-worth. Each day there is a prolific amount of affirmation that being white is OK and an omission of any significant celebration of being Black. This signifies to a child or young person that being Black is somehow less worthy. In addition, racist attitudes continue to permeate the whole of society on a personal and institutional level.

Troyna and Carrington (1990) found recent evidence on individual racism in the United Kingdom suggesting that racial attitudes have remained resilient to change, despite legislative, educational and other reforms. They observe that associations with the violent extremism of the National Front has meant that overt racism has come to be regarded as lying outside the parameters of respectability. So individual racism tends to be more subtle nowadays, and people may deny their own racism by declaring: 'I'm not prejudiced, but ...' (Billig et al, 1988)

The child's way of responding to racial groups other than their own is generally consistent with adult attitudes. As racism becomes established in society its transmission to future generations is affected by its proliferation through the 'majority culture'. As Milner (1983) points out, when racism has taken root in the majority culture and has pervaded its institutions, language, social intercourse and cultural productions, it has entered the very fabric of the society. It reaches all sections of the population including those who are neither objectively nor subjectively threatened by Black people, nor stand to gain anything by discrimination against them. Moreover, the majority culture also retains a history of past race relationships, a history of assumptions and attitudes about Black people, that are influenced by imperialism, colonialism and slavery. This, we feel, maintains the transmission of prejudice to children and young people.

BRITAIN AND ITS PEOPLE: FACTS AND FIGURES

There were Africans in Britain during the Roman occupation. They were soldiers in the Roman army which occupied southern Britain for three and a half centuries. In AD 210 Libyan-born Septimus Severus, Emperor of Rome, arrived to inspect Hadrian's Wall, where a unit of Ethiopians was stationed at Aballava (now Burgh-by-Sands) near Carlisle.

The remains of a young African girl were found in a burial dated c.1000 at North Elmham, Norfolk. (P. Edwards, *Africans in Britain Before 1560*, 1981).

Was Lucy Negro Shakespeare's Dark Lady? Yes, according to GB Harrison's *Shakespeare At Work 1592-1603* (Routledge, 1933). She played the Abbess de Clerkenwell in the Gray's Inn revels of Christmas 1594. 'Abbess' meant Brothel Madam, suggesting that there were Black prostitutes in Elizabethan London.

Henrys VII and VIII employed a Black trumpeter known as John Blanke (White). He earned 8d a day in November 1507.

In 1555 a group of Africans arrived in England from Ghana. They were described as 'tall, strong men (who) could well agree with our kind of food and drink (although) the cold and damp air gives them some trouble'. Their help was needed to break Portugal's trade monopoly in West Africa, and to this end they were taught English and returned as interpreters.

Queen Elizabeth I berated the buccaneer John Hawkyns for trafficking in Black slaves in 1563. She called it 'detestable' and said that it would 'call down the Vengeance of Heaven upon the Undertakers'.

From 1680 to 1686 two million Black slaves captured in Africa passed through British ports en route to America, one third destined for the sugar plantations of Jamaica. The infamous trade continued to enrich many merchants and ports so that when the Commons turned down William Wilberforce's first bill to abolish the slave trade in 1791, Bristol rang its church bells, lit a bonfire, held a fireworks display and gave its workers a half-day holiday. It took another 16 years to bring the slave trade to an end.

Francis Barber was Dr Johnson's Black servant. A visitor witnessed one of the first organised meetings of Black people in Johnson's house in 1760. Johnson scandalised 'some very grave men at Oxford' with the toast: 'Here's to the next insurrection of the negroes in the West Indies.'

Indians first came to England via the East India Company. When William Hickey left India in 1808 he gave 2,000 rupees in farewell presents to his 63 servants, which included two cooks, two bakers, eight waiters, three grass-cutters, four grooms and nine valets.

A Black Drummer in the West Essex Yeomanry Cavalry, disbanded in 1877, had previously served as a member of the Coldstream Guards.

The first Black writer recognised in Britain published an account of his settler life in 1770. He was Ukawsaw Gronniosaw, from Lake Chad, Nigeria.

The first political leader of Britain's Black community was Olaudah Equiano from Eastern Nigeria, who came to England in 1757, aged 12.

IN 1820, on 1 May, two Black radicals were hanged and beheaded for their beliefs. They were on a secret list of 33 leading reformers compiled for the Home Secretary from police reports in 1819.

Mary Seacole, the Jamaican nurse whose reputation rivalled Florence Nightingale's after the Crimean War, was 'cheered and cheered ... by adoring soldiers'. Her autobiography, *The Wonderful Adventures of Mrs Seacole in Many Lands*, was published in 1857 and reissued by Falling Wall Press in 1986.

Raja Rammohan Roy, poet, philosopher, reformer and journalist, was the first Asian to engage in British politics, between 1830-1833, submitting 'the first authentic statement of Indian views' to the Parliamentary Committee on Indian Affairs. Dadabhai Naoroji was the first Asian to be elected to the House of Commons, as Liberal MP for Central Finsbury in 1892.

1917: the first African students' union was founded.

The first effective Black pressure group, the League of Coloured Peoples, was founded by Dr Harold Arundel Moody in 1931. Stella Thomas, another founder member, became the first Black woman to be called to the Bar, in 1933.

Saturday evening, 23 August 1958 saw ninety minutes of fighting between Black people and white in the St Ann's Well Road area of Nottingham. Sensational press reporting whipped up the anti-Black rioting the following weekend when thousands of white people went on the streets shouting: 'Let's get the Blacks.' By the end of October the Notting Hill riots in London were over.

There are more than 140,000 racial attacks in the UK every year.

There are more than 1,000 mosques in Britain and an estimated 10,000-20,000 Muslim converts in the UK. There are 15,000 Muslim doctors in Britain.

Popularly conceived as Black areas? For example, in Brixton, whites make up 60 per cent of the population and Blacks 40 per cent.

Manchester University research found that the ethnic minority population is unlikely ever to rise above 10 per cent of the whole. (*Ethnic Dimensions of the 1991 Census: A Preliminary Report*)

In the north and Scotland just over 1.3% of the population are from ethnic minorities; 8.2% in the West Midlands; 4.8% in the East Midlands; 4.4% in Yorkshire; 1.5% in Wales; while one in ten people in the South-East have African, Caribbean or Asian origins.

London's children speak almost 200 different languages.

53 per cent of the current black Caribbean community were born in the UK and 67,000 people described themselves as 'Black British'.

Minority ethnic groups suffer higher rates of unemployment: Bangladeshis are the hardest hit at 35%; Black Africans 29.6%; Indians 11.8%; Black Caribbean 19%; Chinese 12.5%; as against 10% of whites. (*London's Ethnic Minorities – One City Many Communities*, London Research Study (1994) 81 Black Prince Road, London SE1 7SZ)

Sources: *Staying Power, The History of Black People in Britain* by Peter Fryer, Pluto Press (1984); *Black British, White British* by Dilip Hiro, HarperCollins (1979).

Compiled by Jane Thomas, Observer Life, 28 January, 1996

This chart highlights the fact that the ethnic minority community accounts for 5.5% of the total population in Great Britain.

RESIDENT POPULATION BY ETHNIC GROUP: GREAT BRITAIN 1991
(Thousands, percentage)

ETHNIC GROUP	No.	% of total population	% of total ethnic minority population
All ethnic groups	54,889	100	
White	51,874	94.5	
Ethnic minority groups	3,015	5.5	100.0
Black groups	891	1.6	29.5
Black Caribbean	500	0.9	16.6
Black African	212	0.4	7.0
Black other	178	0.3	5.9
Indian	840	1.5	27.9
Pakistani	477	0.9	15.8
Bangladeshi	163	0.3	5.4
Chinese	157	0.3	5.2
Other groups			
Asian	198	0.4	6.6
Non-Asian	290	0.5	9.6

Source: *OPCS 1991 Census* November 1993, (the first to include a question on ethnic groups).

CHAPTER TWO

SUPPORTING IDENTITY DEVELOPMENT: A THEORETICAL FRAMEWORK

What is Identity?

Identity can be defined as a 'sense of self' (Ryburn, 1992) or, as one young child says: 'you wouldn't be you without it'. All of us have some conception of who or what we are and the formation of this identity is a major area of child development.

> A positive sense of self is crucial to a child's development. All children need to develop a sense of identity and self-worth, which comes through relating positively to family tradition, culture, ethnic and social group, religion, language and gender. Unless children feel thoroughly secure and reasonably free from anxiety, growth in other areas, even their general health can be affected. (*Ensuring Standards* – National Children's Bureau, 1991)

Beverley Prevatt Goldstein (1995) describes the role of identity as twofold: to provide a stabilising, integrated core – an emotional health model – and, secondly, to provide a collective reference point that can be used for group awareness – a political action model.

Traditional theoretical perspectives on identity

Much has been written about identity and its formation and development. Two traditional theoretical perspectives provide a useful backdrop for later discussions about supporting identity development for Black/mixed parentage children and young people.

1. The Symbolic Interaction Approach

This approach is based on the work of CH Cooley and was expanded by GH Mead in the 1930s. Cooley (1902) highlighted the socialised aspect of identity development by arguing that our identity is shaped by the perceptions of those close to us, i.e. significant others. He developed the concept of 'the looking glass self', in which the self is reflected in the reactions of others. In order to define who we are, we need to interpret how other people perceive us and so build a picture of ourselves.

Mead (1934) argues that young children initially develop as social beings by imitating the actions of those around them. For example, in play situations children often imitate what adults do. By the age of four or five, Mead notes that simple imitation will have evolved into more complicated games in which a child will act out an adult role. Mead describes this as taking 'the role of the other'. Children thus achieve an understanding of themselves as separate agents – as a 'me' – by seeing themselves through the eyes of others. Self-awareness is thus achieved when we learn to distinguish the 'me' from the 'I'. The 'I' is the unsocialised infant who reacts with spontaneous wants and desires. The 'me' is the social self. Mead develops Cooley's thesis, that individuals develop self-consciousness by coming to see themselves as others see them. A further stage of development occurs when children are aged eight or nine and learn to grasp what Mead terms the 'generalised other' – the general values and moral rules involved in the culture in which he or she is developing.

Nobels (1973) and Cross (1987) extend the 'I' and 'me' concept to include a perception of being defined as a member of a particular group. Nobles defines this as 'we-ness', and Cross as 'one's reference group'.

2. Erikson's Developmental Approach

Erikson (1963) argues that identity is not static. He describes how each of us constructs a sense of identity in relation to our given characteristics through the process of decision making, choosing particular courses of action within our social environments.

This process is described by Erikson in terms of personal crisis at various stages of our lives. Each stage represents a social conflict for the individual in his/her interaction with others. The way the individual resolves the conflicts is the major determinant of that individual's psychological adjustment. Erikson argues that each individual passes through eight stages:

(1) Trust v basic mistrust

(2) Autonomy v shame and doubt   Early

(3) Initiative v guilt   Childhood

(4) Industry v inferiority

(5) Identity v role diffusion   Adolescence

(6) Intimacy v role diffusion

(7) Generativity v stagnation   Adulthood

(8) Ego identity v despair

According to Erikson, having a positive sense of identity is intrinsically linked with our capacity to meet with and handle situations of crisis and difficulty in our lives. He highlights the importance of the congruence of personal or individual identity and group or communal identities if one is to form a mature, stable and healthy personality.

As Maxime (1986) argues, an eclectic view of the varying theoretical perspectives can aid our interpretation of events, and elements of these approaches are referred to in later discussions.

Influences on Identity Development

Michael Argyle (1969) highlighted four major factors which influence the development of how we perceive ourselves.

(1) **The reaction of others**: As Cooley and Mead highlighted, the reactions of others are a key factor in identity formation. During the early years children's learning about their environment and themselves is significantly influenced by their parents, carers, siblings etc. The child has no frame of reference for evaluating parental reactions – parents are all-powerful figures as far as the young child is concerned, so what they say is fact. Argyle explains this in terms of 'introjection' whereby we come to incorporate into our own personalities the perceptions, attitudes and reactions to ourselves of our carers – and it is through the reactions of others that the child learns what is acceptable.

(2) **Comparison with others**: One way in which we come to form a picture of what we are like is to see how we compare to others. Certain aspects of our self-image only take on significance through comparison, for example, how tall or short we are.

(3) **Social roles**: We incorporate more and more roles into our self-image as we grow up. The young child has familial roles – son, daughter, brother, sister, grandchild. As we grow up our duties and responsibilities as well as our choices involve us in all kinds of roles and relationships with others, for example, occupational roles, groups and organisations we belong to. Social roles provide the societal 'norms' for behaviour.

(4) **Identification**: This area highlights the impact of having positive role models with which people can identify.

In any society where the norms, values and social institutions are not representative of all sections of the community there is likely to be discrimination. When people from ethnic minority groups are excluded from participation on an equal basis, on account of their racial background, there is racism. Racism can create unequal life chances for children and young people.

> The solid foundation on which a building needs to rest can be compared to a person's identity – that inner core which from the beginning must be carefully constructed and maintained. Many children both white and Black are affected by a lack of self esteem but for Black children, including those of mixed parentage, the establishment of ethnic/racial identity, feeling positive about your heritage, culture, this is going to be compounded by racism. Being constantly presented with a white world in which black people are devalued or ignored, they may pick up messages from an early age that to be white is better than to be Black. (EYTARN)

By re-examining Argyle's four factors we begin to see the impact racism can have on children's perceptions of themselves:

(1) **The reaction of others**: How does the media portray Black people, what are the messages Black children pick up about themselves?

'I feel I have to censor what my children watch – it seems the only Black people on prime time television are muggers and drug-dealers on programmes like *The Bill'*. *Christine, a white mother of Black children*

(2) **Comparison with others**: Are Black children compared negatively with others, do we alter our expectations regarding behaviour, achievement etc?

'When I was about seven years old, my mum sat me down and explained things to me. She said it didn't matter if my friends cursed and swore, I could not curse and swear. It didn't matter if I did as well as my friends, I had to do better to achieve the same. It was harsh, but it was reality and I'll always respect my mother for it'. *Peter*

(3) **Social roles**: How prevalent are stereotypes and caricatures of Black people and how much do they impact on behavioural 'norms'?

'I was told that the only thing I was good for was cricket'. *A fifteen year old Black youth, commenting on teacher's advice*

(4) **Identification**: Who are the role models for Black children, are they made aware of the contributions of Black people in a variety of fields throughout history?

'My teacher played us some music by Beethoven and it was really exciting. But my teacher didn't know he was Black like me'. *Jacob, aged six.*

'I love learning about the Egyptians, they're really interesting. But I didn't know they were Africans until my dad told me'. *David, aged seven.*

Early Conceptual Development

According to Milner (1983), white majority group children in a multiracial society show evidence of being aware of simple racial differences from a very early age, sometimes as young as three years old. In the following years they begin to show feelings about these other groups. These evaluations are confirmed by others around them as well as other influences. By the age of about five they may voice these attitudes as they begin to understand the social roles of whites and Blacks. This is likely to reproduce versions of adult stereotypes, thus perpetuating racism.

> Alternative answers or explanations are absent and the child's earliest contacts with the broader universe are filtered through all the biases and distortions in (their) parents' conception of reality. (E.E Jones and H.B. Gerard, 1967)

Louise Derman Sparks suggests that by the age of two, children are learning the appropriate use of gender labels (girl, boy) and learning the names of colours, which they then begin to apply to skin colour.

By three, children are displaying signs of being influenced by societal norms and biases and may exhibit 'pre-prejudice' towards others on the basis of gender or race or having differing abilities.

Between three and five, children try to figure out what are the essential attributes of themselves, which aspects of their identity remain constant, for example:

> Will I always be a girl/boy?
> Can I become a mummy?
> Why am I this colour?

As their self-awareness develops children need a good deal of help to sort through the many experiences and variables of identity.

By the age of four or five children not only engage in gender-appropriate behaviour defined by the socially prevailing norms but they also reinforce it among themselves without adult intervention. Children have already internalised stereotypic gender roles, racial prejudice and a fear of children who have disabilities.

> Our identity incorporates difference – race, gender, sexuality, class etc. either explicitly or implicitly, depending on the context and personal interpretation of the context – whether difference is valued or used to include or exclude is significant. (Beverley Prevatt Goldstein, 1995)

CHAPTER THREE

THE IMPACT OF RACISM ON THE IDENTITY OF CHILDREN AND YOUNG PEOPLE

> My daughter was always confident going to new places – playscheme, gymnastics, swimming. Until one day, at gymnastics, another girl looked at my daughter and her friend and said 'there's lots of monkeys here today'. Since then she doesn't want to go anywhere new. *Sarah*

Research about the impact of racism on children's identity development exposes the damage it can inflict. Milner (1983) compares the responses of five to eight year olds to whom he gave dolls representing various racial groups. The children – classified as Asian, West Indian and White English – were asked, among other questions, 'Which doll looks most like you?' Twenty-four per cent of the Asian children and forty-eight per cent of the West Indian children said they looked more like the white doll than the doll which represented their own racial group. When asked 'If you could be like one of these two dolls, which would you rather be?' sixty-five per cent of the Asian and eighty-two per cent of the West Indian children chose the white doll. The white children, however, all identified with the white doll and chose to be like the white doll.

The adoptive parents of a Black child of mixed parentage, who featured in the BBC's series, *Multiracial Britain,* felt that being brought up in a mixed parentage affluent family would be enough to protect their son Stephen from feeling inferior, an idea being imposed on him by the outside world. At five he was a popular boy looking forward to moving from playgroup to school. On the morning of his first day at school he spent a long time washing his hands. When he emerged from the bathroom it was to show his mother the lighter palms of his dark-skinned hands, saying: 'Look mum, they're not so brown today.' (*Radio Times*, 21.4.79)

Harif Kureishi, author of *My Beautiful Launderette*, was born in London of a Pakistani father and an English mother. He recalled:

> I was desperately embarrassed and afraid of being identified with these loathed aliens. I found it almost impossible to answer questions about where I came from. The word 'Pakistani' had been made into an insult. It was a word I didn't want used about myself. I couldn't tolerate being myself ... I suspected that my white friends were capable of racist insults. And many of them did taunt me innocently. I reckoned that at least every day since I was five years old I had been racially abused. I became incapable of distinguishing between remarks that were genuinely intended to hurt me and those intended as humour. (quoted by Siraj-Blatchford, 1994)

The following is a transcript of part of a conversation between a teacher and a three year old child of mixed 'race' in a predominantly white nursery class in Birmingham. The teacher (DE) was showing the child (A) pictures from a photopack called *Behind the Scenes* (DEC, 1988).

15

DE Do you like this picture?

A They're playing football.

DE Are they playing football, or having a race maybe? What do you think?

A They are playing football, because ..... shorts on.

DE Because of the shorts. Do you like these children? ..... Which one do you like best?

A I don't, I don't like them blackie ones.

DE You don't?

A No, I don't, I like ... (pointing to some white children in the picture) .... They're not winning.

DE No these boys are winning, aren't they, these ones at the front here.

14

A takes another picture to look at.

DE What's happening here?

A Crying

DE Yes, why do you think she's sad? .... Do you think she might be sad because somebody might have called her 'blackie'?

A She is blackie.

DE Yes, but do you think that might make her sad if people called her that? ... Does it make you sad if somebody calls you 'blackie'?

A I, I'm not blackie ....

The fact that this three year old denies being Black and expresses these feelings about 'blackies' reaffirms our earlier assertion. All children in this society, white and Black, grow up with negative images of Black people. Their socialisation into a racist culture comes from a variety of sources. So it is likely that Black children as well as white will internalise the message that it is bad to be Black.

Being fostered

The comments below made by Black children and young people who were fostered or adopted by white families are taken from *It's our right*, SCF/UNICEF – UK (1990):

DAVID

David's mother is white English and his father is Nigerian (Yoruba).

'It's obvious to me that my foster parents wouldn't have been able to bring me up as a Black person. No one ever mentioned anything to me about being Black all the time I was in care. I was always taught in my growing up that Black was bad, and that because I spoke nicely, white people would accept me as being one of them – it doesn't matter about my skin colour, that doesn't matter, blot that out. That is the attitude I was given – and still get.

I think that a lot of my problems when I was a youngster were down to my colour. The reason why I exaggerated my personality when I was a kid was to be noticed as a person, not as they thought I was. I think this was because I didn't know anything about being Black. People used to call me Black bastard, coon, wog and all this kind of stuff, and I didn't know why. Not at that age. My foster parents didn't do a lot for me as far as Black consciousness goes – that's one thing they did absolutely nothing for. They definitely didn't encourage it. They'd make comments that 'everyone's the same' which isn't true. Everyone's different and that needs to be emphasised to us when we're younger otherwise we reject what makes us different and that gets us into a terrible problem when we're older. The worst problem I had in care was an identity problem which nobody who was around at the time could help me with. I feel that Black kids should go into Black families.'

SHARON

Sharon's father is Jamaican and her mother is Irish

'I didn't realise I was Black when I was with my foster parents. The whole area was white. I went to nursery school but there weren't any other Black kids there. I didn't realise I was any different. It was never discussed. After I went to live with my Dad, that's when I found out I wasn't quite white at all. One of my cousins put her arm next to mine and said: 'You're not white, you're Black' and I couldn't cope with it. I was about six. We did get a lot of stick, where we lived in south London when I came back from living with my foster parents. That's when I found I wasn't white and the kids used to call me 'Black bastard'. We just tried to be like them but they wouldn't accept us. I think Black children should go to Black families from the start. The younger the better. I think social services are set up to provide the best care and I don't think a Black child going to live in a white family is the best care for a Black child because a Black child never came from a white family in the first place. As for children of mixed parentage well that's a bit difficult. Some people might say they'd rather be fostered with a mixed parentage family, or a Black family or some even a white family ... I'd say we ought to be fostered with Black people.'

ROSIE

Rosie's mother is white English and her father is of Caribbean or African-American origin. She was 11 at the time of this interview.

'I just realised I was Black, no one told me – I was about two. I don't think it matters having white parents. I think it's just the same. Just different colours. I'm not unhappy to be Black, in fact I'm proud of my colour. I'm quite intelligent but I'm good at sport things ... I don't think that's anything to do with being Black though. There's only two white children in the class but they don't get picked on. I don't know whether I'd rather have Black parents – it depends on what they're like. I don't think it matters. I'm not a half-caste. I'm a whole person. I'm Black.'

Conclusion

Research shows that racism damages the emotional, intellectual and social development of all children. The cumulative effects of discrimination and stereotyping can leave some Black children and young people feeling isolated, angry or rejected (see chart overleaf). It can leave some white children with false notions of superiority and encourage the perpetuation of racism through bullying, name-calling and exclusion. Fundamental concepts of fairness, equality, sharing, co-operation and respect are all distorted. Children are denied the chance to learn and appreciate the aspirations and achievements of others. All those involved are thus being disadvantaged.

White children who harbour feelings of superiority are unable to value the accomplishments of others and black children are restricted by other people's low expectations of them as well as being hurt by such assumptions. (Working Group Against racism in Children's Resources, 1991)

Experiencing Oppression and Discrimination

Dismissive ———————————   ——————————— Ridicule

Patronising ———————————   ——————————— Discounting

Stereotyping ———————————   ——————————— Ignoring

Oppression and Discrimination reinforce stereotypes and justification for this action can be found in comments such as:

'Difficult people'   'Not interested in services'   'They look after themselves'

What happens to the person who experiences this oppression and discrimination?

```
LOSS OF CONFIDENCE
LOSS OF SELF-ESTEEM
HURT
```

NEGATIVE ENERGY
GOING INWARDS

NEGATIVE ENERGY
GOING OUTWARDS

Non-involvement

Anger

Withdrawal

Hostility

Both need **ACTION** – Self-help Challenge Change .

(Gill Howe, Oxfordshire Social Services)

CHAPTER FOUR

THE VALUE OF BLACK IDENTITY – TWO PERSPECTIVES

Many Black people, sociologists and psychologists argue that children in mixed parentage families will benefit if they have a positive Black identity because this will accord with reality – that is, they will be seen and treated as Black by society. A commitment to Black identity, it is argued, is a safeguard against identity confusion and low self-esteem for these children and better equips them to handle racism.

Given the influence of racism, children and young people growing up in mixed parentage families and living in predominantly white neighbourhoods, may find it difficult to develop a positive sense of identity if:

- they have little or no peer group support;

- their carers don't recognise racism is a problem;

- they feel they are required to fit into the society around them, and give up their cultural identity so being unable to take pride in themselves, their families and their culture;

- they deny their Blackness.

Children and young people may need support in accepting all of themselves and feeling comfortable with being Black with a white parent – without support they and their white parent may find it easier to ignore their Black heritage.

Interviewer: Don't you feel it's important for the children to be allowed to form their own identities?

Mother A: I think people ought to understand that we're not trying to get the children to see themselves as Black and only Black and to deny the white side ... Why society sees these children as a problem is because they're coming from parents of two different colours.

Mother B: Positive Black images are so limited in the media. Black images are often limited to the mugger in The Bill . One of my children said something that really bowled me over. He said he wished he was white because white people hate Black people – and that's a terrifying thought for any parent to have to deal with. (Radio Oxford interview, September 1995)

Cross (1987) argues that to understand Black children's identity development, it is necessary to distinguish between personal identity and reference group orientation. The first category includes self-concept factors such as self-esteem, self-confidence and self-evaluation. The second category includes factors such as racial identity, awareness and racial ideology.

From his analysis of studies on Black children, Cross concluded that Black children's personal identity is equal to or surpasses white children's, but that Black children's 'reference group' orientation, i.e. their perceptions of belonging to their racial group, comes out low in many studies and that this impedes Black children's ability to withstand and challenge the damaging impact of racism on their life experiences.

Tizard and Phoenix (1989) argue similarly for a distinction between racial identity and self-concept: 'young Black children can have negative feelings about racial identity and yet have a positive self-concept'. Nick Banks (1992), however, argues that when individuals judge or evaluate their own group attributes using the racist notions of others, they adopt racism and in effect devalue their own racial group and themselves.

Maxime (1986), a Black psychologist, illustrates the crucial importance of racial identity in the positive construction of self, along with all the other affirming experiences necessary to nurture a child's positive image of the self:

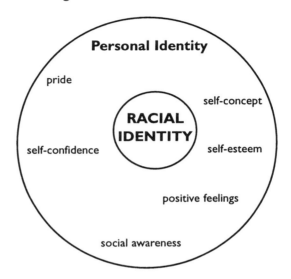

Personal Identity: pride, self-concept, self-esteem, social awareness, positive feelings and self-confidence are all located within the aspect of personal identity. All human beings, regardless of race, gender or culture, need these components to develop a positive sense of self. Racial identity represents the ethnographic dimension of the self.

Racial Identity: Maxime stresses the importance of racial identity in connection with issues such as self-hatred. The nurturance of Black children's development of racial identity is fundamental to sound psychological well-being.

Cross (1971) developed a five-stage model of what he called 'nigrescence' – the process some individuals go through towards a secure and confident Black identity. Maxime has provided a summary of Cross's five stages which characterise a Black person in the process of positive change and provides clinical cases to highlight and explain each stage. These processes can also be related to the stages that white professionals, carers and parents may need to work through in order to begin to redress inherent racism (see page 21).

The Pre-Encounter Stage

At this level, the person's world view is white orientated (eurocentric). She or he will even deny that racism exists. The child's racial self has not been nurtured and their outer and inner realities are not integrated, especially when the outer reality is perceived as negative.

'When I was called names I wondered why I was born like this, why could I not be white; I never wanted to be Black' (from *Working with 'mixed race' young people*, Wayne Richards)

The Encounter Stage

The child or young person now faces experiences or observes a situation that brings them face to face with racism. The experience can be so shattering that it forces them to reinterpret their world. A young girl in therapy projected her rage onto Maxime. As Maxime brought her to a stage of looking at herself as she really was – a Black child – this girl became so frightened of 'herself' that she projected that fear by abusing every Black person she came into contact with.

This stage needs very sensitive handling so that the overt behaviours can be placed in context – focusing on the internal turmoil that the child is experiencing. This young girl is at the point of realisation that her old frame of reference is inappropriate and is slowly moving toward developing a positive Black identity.

The Immersion-Emersion Stage

'This stage encompasses the most sensational aspects of Black identity development' (Cross 1971) and is undoubtedly the most sensitive of the stages. Within this phase the person struggles to remove all semblance of the old identity, while intensifying 'Blackness'. Unfortunately, because the identity process is not positively founded, typical behaviours sometimes include the disparagement of white people and the idolisation of Black people. This could be especially painful for white parents of black children.

When Tina (of Asian and African decent) first came to therapy she wore her hair combed over her face; her eyes were hardly visible (especially the way she hung her head), and her clothes were purposefully pulled to cover all fingers. Once Tina had progressed through the first two stages and entered this one, she reduced her communication to her white carers. One morning she got up and proceeded to paint her entire room black, including the furniture.

Understanding the stage the child is going through is *essential* if we are to aid them through this phase. Individuals can be encouraged to emerge gradually to a more rational position.

The Internalisation Stage

The child or young person has now managed to separate the old identified self and the new self, thus moving towards a positive Black identity. In this stage, they can be assisted to explore race, its impact, its influence and how race relates to them. Care should be taken at this stage to ascertain that those who are at the internalisation stage are not equating a positive Black identity with mistrust of white people and friends. For instance, Paul, a mixed-parentage child who was rejected by his white foster mother after her Black husband left her, worked painfully through the stages but felt that he could not trust white people again. However he did have some caring white friends whom he valued and appreciated. What he found most significant was that he could for the first time love his white friends without at the same time feeling 'bad' about being Black and hating his skin colour. He reported that he was now comfortable for the first time and liked himself as he was.

The Internalisation-Commitment Stage

Here the individual advances on the previous stage by involving her or himself in Black groups or community issues. Paul now extended his network of groups and lost the deep-seated fear that areas where there were many Black people should be avoided at all costs.

Identity resolution (to achieve the internalisation-commitment stage) can occur in at least three ways:

Stagnation – the child's failure to move beyond her or his initial identity state – in fact some young people stagnate at various stages, especially the 'immersion' stage. They could be there for some time unless given help to move on towards identity resolution.

Stage-wise linear progression – there is sequential movement from one identity stage to another.

Recycling – here the child or young person may move back through a stage already completed. Some Black children have found the encounter stage so shattering that they attempt to revert back to the pre-encounter stage.

In Maxime's experience, particularly in the area of fostering and adoption, Black children experiencing problems with their identity were children in the seven to twelve years age group. These are important years in the acquisition of identity development.

In conclusion, Maxime stresses the need for racial identity to be understood by practitioners as well as parents – not only is this a developmental issue which needs to be acknowledged but the effect on one's health, education and psychological well-being needs also to recognised.

(Notes/extracts taken from Chapter 6, Therapeutic Importance of Racial Identity in Working with Black Children Who Hate, Jocelyn Emama Maxime, 1993)

Stages in the thinking that white professionals, carers and parents may need to work through in order to begin to redress their inherent racism

Peake (1996) related Cross's five stage model to a white situation:

Pre-encounter stage

The person's view is white orientated. She/he may deny racism exists. This denial may take the form of 'colour blindness', insisting everyone is the same, or that racism doesn't exist. Inequalities in terms of opportunities available to Black people in society, for example, in housing, employment and education, is due, in their eyes, to the nature and behaviour of Black people.

The Encounter Stage

For white people in a predominantly white culture, the situation that brings them face to face with racism could be a personal friendship with a Black person in which it is realised that not everyone treats your friend as you do. It could also be a high profile situation far removed from oneself, such as the manifest unfairness of the imprisonment of Nelson Mandela, or the acquittal of the white policeman in America who assaulted Rodney King. This experience can be shattering because confrontation of racism at an individual, institutional or societal level indicts white society and, by association, all white people.

The Immersion – Emersion Stage

In this stage, the white person struggles to shake off a Eurocentric view and in their effort, sees all racial minority groups as oppressed and the victims of circumstances. Often behaviour can be excused to an extent that overcompensation for racism becomes irrational. The view can be taken that all white people are racist and Black people are unconditionally to be admired.

The Internalisation Stage

In this stage the white person develops an awareness of race and identity. The person is able to identify factors that have shaped their thinking about Black people. They can now recognise the inaccuracy of their earlier views and acceptance of racial stereotypes and may begin to seek out information about Black people and their history.

The Internalisation-Commitment Stage

In this stage the person understands that to do nothing is to collude with racism and that it is the responsibility of everyone to act against it. Racism is no longer seen as a struggle for Black people alone. The person is now able to take action to challenge racism. This can be done at an individual level by challenging stereotypes, at an institutional level by supporting equal opportunity policies and practices, and at a societal level by promoting knowledge, understanding and respect.

Familial racism

Banks (1992) collected information over a year from a sample of twenty-seven social services clients in the West Midlands and acquaintances of these clients. He looked at the damaging effects on children of mixed parentage if their white mother was angry with the Black father. Although he stresses that it is not his intention to separate or disassociate mixed parentage children from other Black children, he confirms that children of mixed parentage may have differing needs and experiences. Where the Black parent is absent, the children's experiences can be distinct from other Black children's as they lack the opportunity to identify with their ethnic role model.

Banks recognised the damage of 'familial racism' which may arise because of resentment and anger when the Black partner is absent. White mothers of Black children might also be rejected by their family and so lack other support. A number of women in such circumstances admitted that they had not been aware of the social and personal significance of having a Black child. Some had even been congratulated by passers-by for 'fostering' their own child!

Earlier surveys show that feelings ran high concerning interracial liaisons:

45% disapproved of inter-racial marriages (Barton, 1959)

91% disapproved of inter-racial marriages (Hill, 1965)

68% of white fathers were hostile to their daughters marrying a West Indian

75% of white fathers were hostile to their daughters marrying an Indian

77% of white fathers were hostile to their daughters marrying a Pakistani (Wells, 1970).

Banks' work supports his view that 'for psychological consolidation of ethnic self to successfully take place, the child's only viable position will be to support the social reality of how they will be perceived and treated as a way of positively preparing them for the experience of oppression and racism.' In other words, Black children of mixed parentage need to form an identity with which they are comfortable. Some parents and children try to deny their Black identity, as do some professionals. This mismatch with reality can be damaging.

'My mum told me I'm not Black. She says I'm white because my skin's not much darker than hers. But I know I'm not white because my dad's Black.' *David, aged 6*

According to Goldstein (1995):

Black children with a white parent are already likely to experience racism. It seems essential that they are offered the opportunity to benefit from the richness of the image and identity perspectives, to benefit from being members of a group struggle for justice. Black children with a white parent need to feel not only comfortable with a Black identity but able to include in it their particular experience. This seems likely if we can open up a Black identity away from the narrow boundaries of shades of colour or cultural artifacts, if in inviting black children to share this identity we create space for particular self-definitions, multiple identities, varied perspectives and a shared journey towards justice ... Our fixation with shades of colour is unhelpful. I would suggest, as a counterpoint, this verse by Elean Thomas:

> 'Black is not a colour
> It is a statement
> of a shared past
> a present reality
> a future intent.'

If we are to support all children and young people and their families so that our involvement in their care is conducive to their achieving their full potential, we need to consider how this can be put into practice. The following chapters offer practical approaches and strategies.

PART TWO
Successful strategies for supporting children and young people

CHAPTER FIVE

COPING WITH RACIST INCIDENTS

All children and young people should feel valued and be helped to value each other. Before we can help them to value themselves we need to look at our own values and make sure that we do not harbour racist attitudes and prejudices. It may be that some of us will need help in exploring some of these issues. The training ideas set out here are designed to provide some of this help.

Racism is damaging to all the children and young people we care for, white or Black, and it is our responsibility to help them cope with racist incidents in playground, classroom, street, or residential home. Some staff may find this difficult however, because of:

— failing to recognise such incidents

— failing to attribute due importance to racial incidents

— lacking confidence about how to handle incidents – what to say or do

— holding racist views themselves

— not wanting to 'make an issue' over the incident

— embarrassment.

Research by Tizard and Phoenix (1993) indicates that Black children of mixed parentage had no illusions that having a white parent would enable them to escape from racism. They knew they would have to deal with it. Tizard and Phoenix identified basic types of survival/coping strategies children used in threatening situations.

Children attempted to reduce the pain and avoid physical harm by modifying the way they felt about it, for example:

– not noticing the threat, diverting their attention from it, deliberately ignoring it

– discounting the abuse because the abusers are stupid and ignorant

– humbling its user

– treating it as a joke.

Children tackled situations directly by, for example:

– negotiating, defusing through humour, joining with others to tackle it or appealing to adults for support.

Children would take steps to prevent or reduce the effects of the threat by, for example:

– learning self-defence;

– joining with others.

Tizard and Phoenix found that the lack of support added to many young people's distress:

> There's no point ever telling the teachers any more when things happen because they don't do anything about it. They don't even believe me. *Jade, aged 10*

Where carers and staff hold racist views themselves it is important to look at where these damaging views came from and how they have continued to be perpetuated.

Children and young people who are called names, who are excluded or made to feel they are not acceptable, experience a range of emotions – they may feel hurt, humiliated, angry, frustrated and isolated. If they seek the support of an adult and it is not given, these emotions can only be compounded. Recognition of such incidents is vital and so is support to the child or young person concerned.

The children who behave in a racist way can be led to believe that such behaviour is acceptable, if nothing is done about it. It must be made clear to them that racist behaviour is never acceptable.

Some of the effects of racism on Black/mixed parentage children and young people have been found to be feelings of rejection, bewilderment, frustration, sadness, withdrawal, anger. They can be made to feel ashamed of skin colour, hair, language etc. or unprepared for the 'outside' world, i.e. feel unable to cope with racism. Racism can lead to a lack of a positive self-esteem and a lack of motivation/achievement due to the low expectations that are held of them.

White children, too, can be affected adversely. Racism can lead to a feeling of superiority reinforced by a lack of positive Black images. They might grow to be uncaring. Their learning can become blinkered/insular. There is the danger that they, too, will learn to become racist, thus perpetuating racism. Concepts of fairness, equality, justice and respect can become distorted.

A supportive approach can help children and young people to appreciate the impact of their words and actions. It can encourage children to have respect for one another and enable them to stand up for themselves and others.

The following steps should be taken whenever there is a racist incident:

– be clear that you do not accept or collude with the racist statement

– make the recipient of the racism feel that they are valued and that the incident is being taken seriously

- create an environment where the recipient feels comfortable and able to talk to you

- do not 'ignore' the fact that they have a different colour skin – they have

- help the child to feel positive about having a different skin colour, hair etc. Use positive words that make them feel good

- listen carefully to the child's comments, questions, frustrations

- do not deflect their concerns, give truthful explanations

- acknowledge the child's feelings of sadness, confusion, anger, hurt, etc

- point out that people are visibly different in many ways, such as their different eye or hair colour, and that all people should be equally valued

- describe examples of what happened to you in the past when you were made to feel different, and say how you felt

- if you are in the company of the child or young person who was being racist, ask them why they said what they did

- make sure that the perpetrator of the racism is also counselled and not simply made to feel rejected

- make sure that the parents/carers are aware of the incident and how it is being dealt with

- take up the issue with the teacher. Make sure you ask for help and support from others who are working with the children concerned.

CHAPTER SIX

SUPPORTING CHILDREN'S IDENTITY AND SELF-WORTH

By enabling all children and young people to value and respect each other we can reduce feelings of superiority and the ridiculing of others, and promote self-respect and respect for others. The following approaches have been found to be effective:

- Introduce activities, resources and discussions that can build positive racial and cultural self-identity and develop positive attitudes towards people of differing racial and cultural groups, that is, talk about and use factual information in relation to skin tones and hair textures. Don't gloss over physical differences between people.

- Listen carefully to children's questions and comments and make sure you understand what these mean and what the children want to know. It is important to give truthful explanations appropriate to children's level of understanding. If you don't feel confident to answer at once, tell the children so and try to give them an answer later.

- All children need to feel wanted and valued and to be presented with positive images of people and situations with which they can identify. Children of mixed parentage, like all children, are different from each other, and so are their families. Resources that portray stereotypical images should be avoided.

- Build partnerships with parents. Value and respect the range of child-rearing practices, showing your recognition that there are many effective ways of fostering development.

- Be sensitive to the need of children of mixed parentage to define their own identity. We need to ensure that our attitudes and practice values Blackness and that our resources reflect this commitment.

- Pronounce and spell all names correctly. They are closely linked to our identity. A famous man tells of his experience:

On the first day of school my teacher Miss Mdingane, gave each of us an English name and said that thenceforth that was the name we would answer to in the school. This was the custom among Africans in those days and was undoubtedly due to the British bias of our education. The education I received was a British education in which British ideas, British culture and British institutions were automatically assumed to be superior. There was no such thing as African culture ... whites were either unable or unwilling to pronounce an African name and considered it uncivilised to have one. That day Miss Mdingane told me that my new name was Nelson. ((Rolihlahla) Nelson Mandela, *Long Walk to Freedom*, 1994)

To encourage confidence we need to relate to each child so that they feel cared for and important. Every child needs praise, encouragement, support, individual attention and opportunities to experience success and approval.

Our goal should be to help children develop a confident self and group identity, to teach them how to challenge prejudice and to enable them to stand up for themselves and others in the face of injustice. (EYTARN, *The Best of Both Worlds – Celebrating Mixed Parentage,* 1995)

EVALUATING OUR RESOURCES

The *Working Group Against Racism in Children's Resources* (1990) highlighted the need to be alert to all the implications of the materials we offer while attempting to provide an enriching environment for all children. They suggest the following framework by which to evaluate resources:

Stereotyping

There appear to be two main forms of stereotype: i) over-simplified generalisation about a particular group which usually carries derogatory implications; ii) assuming that an individual has particular characteristics (which may or may not be correct) and generalising from that to apply it to all members of that group, for example, 'Asian women are docile'.

Caricature

Exaggerating a characteristic or assumed characteristic which often carries overtones of ridicule. Their physical features, characteristics or clothes are so exaggerated that the person portrayed ceases to be a real person and becomes unreal, a joke, or appears stupid or ridiculous. The 'golliwog' figure is one example.

Tokensim

When 'different' people or their style of clothing are included in an illustration, but their presence is hardly acknowledged in the text, this treatment is tokenistic. If Black people are included in pictures almost as an afterthought, in the background or in unimportant roles, and never as main characters or doing important things, they are being marginalised and the effect is tokenistic.

Incorrect names

Naming people correctly is important. People should not be given abbreviated or nicknames just because their names are thought difficult to pronounce. People's names are a fundamental part of them and should be recognised as such.

Undermining of identity

To have a positive identity one must have a positive self-image. Seek out resources (they *are* available) that offer positive images of characters from the groups to which the children belong and of people, situations and events which are recognisably part of their history and way of life.

EVALUATING OUR PRACTICE

Even when all our toys, books and other learning materials have been carefully chosen, *the critical issue is how they are used*. We parents, childcare workers, teachers and trainers need to examine and monitor our own attitudes and feelings, develop our own awareness and commitment to countering racism and be willing to discuss racial and cultural differences openly and to increase our knowledge of various cultures, languages and religions. Otherwise we can well transmit negative messages about children, their families and their way of life.

The following checklist is based on one developed by EYTARN (1995):

- Do adults actively intervene if children/young people are laughed at, injured or excluded because of the colour of their skin, their physical features or the language they speak? This is important because physical abuse, being called names and being ostracised are the experiences of racism most common among children. (*see chapter five of this book: Coping with Racist Incidents.*)

'When I get up and I go to school, if somebody calls me names I feel miserable for the rest of the day'. *Laura, aged 10*

- Are children/young people encouraged to ask questions about physical and cultural differences and are these answered honestly and not ignored or side-stepped by saying 'all people are alike' or 'colour doesn't matter'? Answers like these deny differences and could convey a message that being different is something to be ashamed of.

- Do the resources reinforce or challenge racist and sexist stereotypical thinking? For example, are Black women and men portrayed in a wide variety of occupational roles or in only stereotypical ones?

- Do the books offer all children/young people the opportunity to identify with positive Black, mixed parentage and white characters in leading roles and to see Black adults and children, and those of mixed parentage, portrayed in a non-tokenistic way, as living happy and successful lives?

- Do the resources provided expand children's horizons, communication skills, general knowledge and understanding of the world around them? Do objects used in domestic play represent the range of communities living in Britain?

- Are the dolls, puppets and other models of people provided, accurate and realistic?

- Do the children often have the opportunity of hearing, seeing and using their other languages besides English?

- Do all the parents feel comfortable and relaxed in the environment that has been created for their children?

- Does the environment reflect a range of different cultural backgrounds?

- Are parents encouraged to come in often and share their skills with the children?

- Is there an effective and comprehensive anti-racist policy and is it constantly being evaluated by staff and parents?

- Are on-going training opportunities available for everyone involved with children/young people and their families, including caretakers, foster parents, secretaries, cooks and people who serve the food? This is important because everybody needs to be able to update their skills regularly, evaluate their practice and examine their own attitudes and feelings.

- Do parents, staff, foster parents have knowledge of the community networks/organisations that support Black/ mixed parentage children and young people, or know where to obtain this information?

- Do parents, staff, foster parents have practical information about how to care for the hair/skin care needs of Black/ mixed parentage children and young people, or know where to obtain such information?

This approach is designed to ensure that each child is helped to feel secure, to experience success, to develop self-esteem and to learn a range of intellectual, social and physical skills in an environment in which they and their families are welcomed, valued and comfortable.

PART THREE
Training exercises for workers with children and young people

PRACTICAL TRAINING IDEAS THAT SUPPORT ANTI-RACIST APPROACHES

The following exercises are intended for use by practitioners in social services but can be adapted for use in other settings like schools, youth projects etc. Used together with other sections of this manual, they can provide a day's training for practitioners. Some of the exercises are also appropriate for use with young people.

The aim is to help participants to become more sensitive to the needs of the Black/mixed parentage children and young people with whom they work. Begin by exploring how to recognise and challenge racism; how attitudes are formed and permeate society, and consider the importance of language and, through discussion, the importance of respecting and valuing the diversity of the people we work with.

The exercises can only be effective where there is trust, openness and a willingness to listen and learn. The participants should not be afraid to speak out or make mistakes.

We hope that participants find them useful.

1. WHERE IS THE POWER?

Integral to inequality is the notion of power. Where people are in terms of their employment status denotes what power they have.

Aim

To provide participants with a task as they arrive for the training session.

To help participants to recognise the levels of inequality in the work force and the lack of power for Black people.

What you need

Power grid sheet (to be photocopied)

The statistics (either copied for handouts or prepared on flipchart paper) – not to be shown or given out until everyone has completed the grid.

Time

(30 minutes)

What to do

Give out the grid to each participant as they arrive.

Ask them to find a seat and complete the grid by ticking the appropriate columns. It is important that they do not spend too much time thinking about it. They should be encouraged to think about their own experience – where they bank, shop, go to the doctor etc. and who they encounter in these different roles.

Allow time for participants to complete the grid. (no more than 15 minutes)

Display the statistics on page 41 and invite comments. Does this confirm what they already knew? Does it surprise them? Allow 15 minutes for discussion.

Advice

These statistics show that, in general terms, members of minority ethnic groups are employed in less skilled jobs, at lower job levels and are concentrated in particular industrial sectors. 'A number of studies (Leicester City Council,1990; McCormick, 1988; Pinani et al 1992) have suggested that the pattern revealed by Brown, 1984 has continued into the late 1980s and 1990s.' (Mason, 1995)

JOB LEVELS OF EMPLOYEES

1982 (column percentages)

	Men			Women		
	White	African-Caribbean	Asian	White	African Caribbean	Asian
Professional employer/manager	19	5	13	7	1	5
Other non-manual	23	10	13	55	52	35
Skilled manual/ manual supervisor	42	48	33	5	4	8
Semi-skilled and unskilled manual	16	35	40	32	43	51
Total	100	100	100	100	100	100

JOB LEVELS OF EMPLOYEES IN INDUSTRY AND MANUFACTURING 1982 (column percentages)

	Men			Women		
	White	African-Caribbean	Asian	White	African Caribbean	Asian
Professional employer/manager	13	3	5	6	-	1
Other non-manual	15	2	4	35	19	6
Manual supervisor	13	9	5	2	3	2
Skilled manual	40	43	32	17	13	9
Semi-skilled and unskilled manual	17	43	53	38	65	82
Total (all employees in engineering, vehicles, shipbuilding, manufacturing and mining)	100	100	100	100	100	100

(Source: Brown, 1984)

WHERE IS THE POWER?

	Male	Female	Black	White
Supermarket manager				
Bus driver				
Chair: School Governors				
Road sweeper				
Head of college				
Cleaner				
Bank manager				
Nurse				
Member of Parliament				
Hospital porter				
Council leader				
Factory worker				
Chief Education Officer				
Cashier – Supermarket				
Police Superintendent				

Tick the appropriate columns which represents your experience – where you shop, go to the bank, go to the doctor etc.

2. RESPECTING DIFFERENCES

Aim

To help all participants to engage in discussion.

To help 'set the scene' for the training exercises by encouraging participants to think about a time when they have experienced feelings of unfairness or exclusion in their own lives.

To help participants explore how they have felt being an 'other'.

To help participants to understand how it feels to be considered 'other'.

No equipment needed.

Time

(total 30 minutes)

3 minutes working individually

7 minutes discussion in pairs

20 minutes for feedback in larger group and discussion.

What to do

Ask each participant to think of a situation when they have experienced being an 'other'; when they have felt excluded, an outsider or different.

Ask them to think about how this made them feel. If some participants are lucky enough not to have had direct personal experience of this then ask them to think of a situation where they have noticed it happening to someone else.

When everyone has thought of an incident ask them to share with the person sitting next to them what happened and how they felt about it.

After 10 minutes ask participants to share their experiences with the rest of the group.

3. AGREE/DISAGREE 'CARD' GAME

Aim

To give participants an opportunity to air their views.

To show how attitudes are formed and how prejudice can be challenged.

To challenge attitudes that are offensive.

What you need

Statement 'cards'

Three large sheets of paper headed: *Agree, Disagree or Don't know*, on which to place cards.

Time

30 minutes.

What to do

Photocopy page 43 (ideally onto card) and cut out so that each statement is a single card.

Share these out equally with the group. In turn, each person reads out a statement and decides whether they agree, disagree or don't know. They place their 'card' accordingly, on one of the three piles labelled *Agree, Disagree or Don't Know*.

When all the cards have been put in place, participants discuss each card's placing. Only the person who originally placed the card can move it if the discussion has convinced them that another category is more appropriate.

Advice

Although everyone is entitled to their opinions, some opinions might be offensive to others in the group and to people we work with. Situations of this kind will need to be dealt with sensitively. Opinions might also be expressed that are unacceptable to the department you work in and this will need to be made clear to participants.

(Exercise from *One World – A Race and Culture Activity pack*. Reproduced with permission of the National Youth Agency, Leicester.)

Racist jokes are good for a laugh.	There is no racism in Britain now. We are all equal.	I take no notice of race, I treat everybody the same.	Black people are just as prejudiced against whites as whites are against blacks.	Black people always feel they are being discriminated against, they have big chips on their shoulders.
Those black people who wear western dress are more easily accepted by whites.	Different cultures should not try to integrate with each other.	People should stay in their own countries.	The mass media create racist stereotypes.	The police treat people of different races the same.
	Black people don't have the education necessary to get a good job.	Black parents are very strict.	Children are not prejudiced.	Race relations organisations such as the Commission for Racial Equality, were set up for black people only.

4. MATCH THE MEANING

Aim

To promote an understanding of the language, concepts and terms regularly used in training about race and cultural diversity.

What you need

The 'cards' of terms and meanings.

Time

5-8 minutes for the game and 15 minutes for the discussion.

What to do

Photocopy the page of 'Terms and meanings' and cut out the individual 'cards'. Hand out one card to each member of the group. If there are less than twenty participants make sure that all the cards handed out correspond.

Everyone then walks around the room shouting out the word on their card, trying to match each term with the correct meaning. Once they think they have found their partner, the pair sit down together.

When everyone is in pairs, each set of matched cards is read out loud to the rest of the group. Only when this process is complete does the facilitator check the correct meaning against the list. Any participants with wrong partners should try again to match cards.

When all the cards have been correctly matched, allow time for feedback and discussion on the terms and meanings.

Advice

Pairs should be matched quickly but it may be necessary to set a short time limit, for example, two minutes to find your partner and sit down. By the end all members should have an understanding of what each term means.

(Exercise from *One World – A Race and Culture Activity pack.* Reproduced with permission of the National Youth Agency, Leicester.)

CULTURE	EMIGRANTS
CUSTOM	DISCRIMINATION
RACISM	REFUGEE
XENOPHOBIA	STEREOTYPE
PREJUDICE	IMMIGRATE

Socially transmitted behaviour relating to arts, beliefs, institutions and characteristics of a community, race or nation.	People leaving their native country to settle in another.
Long established habits or traditions of a society followed as a matter of course.	The attitude, behaviour or treatment based on prejudice.
The belief that certain races, especially one's own, are superior to others.	A person who has fled from danger, often war or political persecution.
Hatred or fear of foreign ideas, politics and cultures.	An identification of one group, (or member of a group) by another, based on assumptions, not evidence, but nonetheless. Fixed.
An opinion or judgement formed without knowledge or understanding of the facts.	To enter and settle in a country of which one is not a native.

Match the Meaning: Words and Meanings

Xenophobia
Hatred or fear of foreign ideas, politics and cultures.

Racism
The belief that certain races, especially one's own, are superior to others.

Stereotype
An identification of one group (or member of a group) by another, based on assumptions, not evidence, but nonetheless fixed.

Culture
Socially transmitted behaviour relating to arts, beliefs, institutions and characteristics of a community, race or nation.

Prejudice
An opinion or judgement formed without knowledge or understanding of the facts.

Discrimination
The attitude, behaviour or treatment based on prejudice.

Immigrate
To enter and settle in a country of which one is not a native.

Emigrants
People leaving their native country to settle in another.

Custom
Long established habits or traditions of a society followed as a matter of course.

Refugee
A person who has fled from danger, often war or political persecution.

CASE STUDY – JOE'S STORY

Young black people report widespread and persistent racial harassment from other young people, children and teachers. (Kelly and Cohn, 1988)

Often adults who work with children and young people are unprepared for racist incidents and do not know how best to deal with them. They sometimes collude with them by not challenging the incident, or diminish the importance of the incident by singling out the person being harassed instead of identifying and dealing with the aggressors.

Aim

To get participants to think about how they would deal with an incident of racism in their residential home. The scenario could very easily be adapted to a youth club, school classroom or playground. It is intended to stimulate discussion around:

- recognising the existence of racism

- working out ways of tackling racism

- working out how to move the issue forward in their home, school etc.

What you need

Photocopies of Joe's story
Flip chart and pens

Time

One hour

What to do

Distribute a copy of the scenario to each participant.
Divide into groups of four to six.
Each group selects one person to write on the flip chart and report back to the larger group.
Allow a few minutes for participants to go through the scenario.

Consider each question as a group.
Facilitate all group members to take part in discussion.
Work in groups for 30 minutes.
Report back to the larger group for a further 30 minutes.

Scenario: Joe's Story

Joe is a Black youth who has been accommodated in your residential home.

After the second week he has complained to Tim, the shift leader, about being subjected to racist jokes from some of the white residents and persistently being called derogatory names.

Tim knows the other boys quite well and feels that the 'joking' is not vicious. He tells Joe that he must learn to put up with a little leg-pulling, like everyone else. This precipitates a row and Joe storms out.

Tim later tells one of his colleagues that Joe takes it too seriously. 'He's a nice lad but he's got a chip on his shoulder. He'll have to put up with this if he's going to rub along with everyone else'.

* *

(1) You are unhappy with Tim's handling of the situation but since you are only a casual worker, how can you bring up the incident with him and suggest a better way of dealing with such incidents?

(2) What action should be taken now?

    (a)   with regard to Joe?

    (b)   with regard to the white members of staff and residents of the unit?

(3) How would you ensure that such incidents do not happen again in the home?

WHAT DO WHITE PEOPLE SAY ABOUT BLACK PEOPLE

Aim

To explore the existing images and stereotypes of Black people.

To identify how white people come to think about Black people in certain ways.

To explore what people believe and how this compares with reality.

To think about how to challenge stereotypes and images.

What you need

Large piece of paper and coloured felt tip pens.

Time

35 minutes

What to do

Divide the paper into four quarters with a felt tip pen. (Alternatively, the group can be divided into four groups with each group focusing on one of the subjects listed below.)

Put the title '*What do white people say about Black people*' along the top. In each of the four sections write: media; friends; teachers/ employers; parents/carers.

Ask participants to think about what they have heard said about Black people and write it up on the paper.

Participants consider which statements are positive and which are negative and the reasons for any imbalance. Ask participants to consider the following:

(a) With what do you agree or disagree and why

(b) Would you feel able to challenge the negative stereotypes and images of Black people?

(c) Can these stereotypes affect our friendships or relationships?

Advice

Encourage the participants to be open and honest without being offensive. Other ground rules may be necessary. Help them to think about where they get their opinions from.

(adapted from activity in *The Equaliser II*, Bread Youth Project)

PART FOUR
Activities for children

The following activities are designed for working directly with children, enabling them to think about their own characteristics, what makes them unique, what they have in common with others etc. These activities can be used in small group settings.

ACTIVITY ONE – THE NAME GAME

Aim

This activity enables children to think about what makes them who they are. It can be used as a way of highlighting individuality and how unique each of us is. It can contribute towards building self-esteem and personal development by talking about how we perceive ourselves and comparing this with how others see us.

What you need

A piece of paper and a pen or pencil for each participant.

What to do

Ask everyone to write their name vertically. They can use their first name, surname, nickname or full name. They should use each letter to start a word or short phrase which they feel describes them. If it is very difficult they can use the letter as the last letter of the word instead of the first.

It may be helpful if the adult in the group begins by composing an acrostic using their own name as an example. Or you can use this acrostic by a ten year old, quoted by Robin Richardson:

Rather good at maths

Always working hard

Charming in all my ways

Happy most of the time

Excited by parties

Learning to be strong.

(Richardson: *Fortunes and Fables*, Trentham Books, 1996)

Additional Information

This activity can be adapted for young children, by suggesting that they use the letters of their name to think about things they like. For example:

S – Sun	L – Laughing	C – Cheerful
a – Apples	a – Artist	a – Actress
r – Running	u – Upset sometimes	t – Talkative
a – Animals	r – Running	h – Helpful
h – Home	a – Attractive	y – Young
Sarah, aged 4	*Laura, aged 8*	*Cathy, aged 10*

ACTIVITY TWO – ME

Aim

This activity encourages children to start thinking about the range of factors that combine to make everyone unique. While helping children identify those characteristics that make them distinctive individuals, it can also be used to reveal how much they have in common with others, both in their immediate neighbourhood and with children around the world.

What you need

A piece of paper and a pencil or pen for each participant.

What to do

Ask participants to think of things that make them unique and things they have in common with their friends (if the children are working in pairs, what they have in common with their partners), in common with neighbours and in common with other children around the world.

Additional information

This activity highlights how complex identity is. While there are many characteristics we share with others, it is the precise way in which they are combined in us that makes each of us unique. For example:

I am unique because there is no one the same as me.

The things I have in common with everyone else is I'm human and I breathe.

Rory, aged 12

ACTIVITY THREE – FEELINGS

This activity can be done with an individual child or a group of children.

Aim

To help (young) children become aware of their own feelings and the feelings of others
To help children to understand what it means to be an individual
To help children to express their feelings.

What you need

Two pieces of card with pictures on for each child, one depicting a happy face and one a sad face.

What to do

The children sit in a circle. Each is given the two flash cards, of a happy face and a sad face.

Ask a series of questions (see below) and ask the children to respond by holding up the card that represents how they feel.

Questions

How do you feel when someone pushes you?
How do you feel when you feel unwell?
How do you feel when someone tells you they don't like you?
How do you feel when someone calls you names?
How do you feel about the dark?
How do you feel when someone gives you a birthday present?
How do you feel when someone laughs at you?
How do you feel when you go on holiday?

Discussion

Through discussion, help the child(ren) to think about happy feelings and sad feelings and how they may say or do things that make others sad or happy. How does this make them feel? What can they do or say to make a friend feel happier? How would they like their friends to treat them?

ACTIVITY FOUR – BEING DIFFERENT AND THE SAME

This activity can be done one to one or with a group.

Aim

To help children explore what makes them different and the same
To value their own and one another's social/cultural background
To imagine what it is like to be 'different'
To help children understand that whatever we look like on the outside we all share the same sort of feelings inside.

What to do

Ask the child(ren) to think of three things that make them the same, for example, eye colour; hair; shoes etc. (If working with only one child, use photographs of different children.)

Ask the children to think of three things that make them different

Help the children to share their ideas of what makes them the same and what makes them different.

Advice

Throughout this activity it is important for children to be encouraged to recognise the value and worth of other colour skin, hair etc. Ask them to think of other people, for example, parents, friends, neighbours, who are different in some way.

ACTIVITY FIVE – DOTS ON FOREHEADS

Aim

This activity aims to give children some idea of what it is like to be unpleasantly dominated by someone else. This is obviously not an agreeable experience, and the activity must be handled carefully, but it is important that children understand what it feels like to have power used against them. Some children in the group may already know this only too well, and this should be taken into account when deciding how and when to use this activity. It may be useful if the children have previously considered the ways one group can dominate another, for example, how boys can dominate girls.

What you need

Sheets of sticky dots in *three different colours* (red, blue and green for example).

Time

1 hour 15 minutes

What to do

Ask the children to stand in a circle facing outwards, with their eyes shut. Stick a dot on the forehead of each child so that the colours are evenly distributed.

When every child has a dot on their forehead, ask them to open their eyes, face inwards and get into groups according to the colour of their dots.

Once they have sorted themselves into three groups, ask the group with red dots to stand *silently* in the corner with their noses touching the wall – they must not move until told to. The group with blue dots should be invited to sit down comfortably on chairs. This group can give any order they want to the group with green dots, and the group with green dots *must silently obey*. The group in charge can ask them to mime simple tasks, do animal impressions, serve them a drink and biscuit etc. As long as these requests are not dangerous, they *must* be obeyed silently and promptly.

After a few minutes, stop the children and tell them that a terrible mistake has been made. In fact, the group with blue dots should be standing in the corner, the group with green dots should be sitting down, and the group with red dots should be obeying the group with green dots. Then continue as before.

After a few minutes more, stop the children again and announce that we've got it wrong again! In fact, the real situation should be the green dots standing in the corner, the red dots sitting down, and the blue dots obeying the red dots!

Allow the exercise to continue for a few more minutes and then bring it to a close and discuss it:

- How did each group feel when they were in each position?

- Did they feel badly treated or angry? Did they enjoy giving orders?

- Did they see the people in the other groups as friends or enemies?

- Is it fair that one group of people can dominate another group in such a way? How would the children prefer to work: by dominating or co-operating?

SUMMARY

Scenario A
RED DOTS:
Stand silently in the corner with their noses touching the wall

BLUE DOTS:
Sit down and give orders to GREEN DOTS

GREEN DOTS:
Silently obey orders from BLUE DOTS

Scenario B
BLUE DOTS:
Stand silently in the corner with their noses touching the wall

GREEN DOTS:
Sit down and give orders to RED DOTS

RED DOTS:
Silently obey orders from GREEN DOTS

Scenario C
GREEN DOTS:
Stand silently in the corner with their noses touching the wall

RED DOTS:
Sit down and give orders to BLUE DOTS

BLUE DOTS:
Silently obey orders from RED DOTS.

ACTIVITY SIX – DON'T CALL ME NAMES!

Aim

To discuss racism and how to tackle it, by using drama to examine one aspect of racism – racist abuse.

Advice

It is important that this drama does not reinforce the racist experiences that the Black children have already had to face. It may be best if Black children work together to prepare their drama.

What you need

Photocopies of the scenario *Don't Call Me Names!*

Time

Approximately 1 hour 45 minutes with a group of 24 children

What to do

It is important to introduce the subject to the children in a way that makes sense to them, perhaps by referring back to the *Dots on Foreheads* activity:

How did they feel when they were being ordered about by other people? Angry? Frustrated?

Do the children feel that they are ever treated like that in real life? If so, when?

Point out that in Britain Black people can be dominated by white people in similar ways. Black people are far more likely to be attacked in the street than white people. Black people find it much harder to get a job or a house because they are discriminated against. Often Black people have to face abuse and name-calling. The following activity uses drama to explore this.

Divide the children into small groups.

Give each group a copy of the scenario. Once they have read it they should decide as a group what should happen next and how to act out the completed scenario. This process of discussing the outcome and working out the drama ideas should involve everyone in the group. They have 15-20 minutes to work out the drama so that they can present it to the other groups.

The discussion can be prompted by questions such as:

- What do they think of the story – what feeling does it give them?
- What do they think of the boys' behaviour?
- How would they feel if they were the girl?

Each group can first act out the scenario on page 55. Then they can work out their own ending:

- How should the scenario end?
- How should the girl react to the boys?
- What should the other children in the park do?

After 15-20 minutes ask all the groups to come back together. Ask each group to perform their drama, with the ending they have decided. Make sure that the groups who are watching treat the drama seriously and with respect.

After all the groups have performed, it is important to discuss the children's reactions:

- Did any of the groups choose the same ending?
- If there were differences in the endings, what did they think of the other groups' endings? Did they agree with them, or disagree?
- Why did each group choose the ending that they did?
- Do all the children agree that racist name-calling and abuse is *always* wrong and unjustified?

(Activity Five and Six have been adapted from *Getting on with others: A resource pack on development education for youth work with 6-9 year olds*, The Woodcraft Folk)

SCENARIO – Don't call me names !

It's a nice summer evening, and all the local children are out playing in the park. Everyone is happily playing and enjoying themselves until two boys start to pick on a girl just because she is Black. The boys call her horrible names and say nasty things like 'You lot smell, and you cause all our problems. You should go back to where you come from.'

The girl finds this very upsetting. She knows that she is not smelly, and that she has never caused problems for anyone. She certainly doesn't know where 'to go back to', because she was born only half a mile away and has lived here all her life.

The boys carry on calling her horrible names until .....

ORGANISATIONS AND SUPPLIERS THAT SUPPORT ANTI-RACIST APPROACHES

The following is a list of useful contacts for further information, activities, ideas and materials. We are aware that this kind of list can never be fully comprehensive but it provides a useful starting point for those wishing to take the issues raised in this manual into their working and personal lives. For the address of your nearest 'Multicultural' Resource Centre, contact your local library, Education Department or Social Services.

ACORN PERCUSSION have a wide range of instruments, to suit all age groups and abilities from pre-school to 16 plus, including special needs. Their address is Unit 33, Abbey Business Centre, Ingate Place, London SW8. Telephone: 0171 720 2243

AFFRO COMMUNITY RESOURCES CENTRE
Telephone: 0121 456 3825

ANTI-RACIST TEACHER EDUCATION NETWORK (ARTEN) c/o Samidha Garg, 28 Sandish Edge, London Road, Hemel Hempstead HB3 9SZ

BANGLADESH CENTRE OF EAST LONDON stocks a range of dolls, toys, books, handicrafts, musical instruments and clothing, reflecting the history and culture of Bangladesh. Their address is 185a Cannon Street Road, London E1 2LX

BIRMINGHAM DEVELOPMENT EDUCATION CENTRE Selly Oak Colleges, Bristol Road, Birmingham B29 6LE offer a range of relevant resources and produce a catalogue of current publications. *Where it really matters* is one of their excellent publications.

BLACK CHILDCARE NETWORK 17 Brown Hill Road, London SE6 2ES

BLACK RIVER BOOKS publish and stock children's books, greeting cards, posters and framed/unframed prints, black dolls, puzzles. At 113 Stokes Croft, Bristol BS1 3RW. Telephone: 0117 9423 804 Fax: 9073310

CHILDREN IN SCOTLAND 5 Shandwick Place, Edinburgh EH2 4RG. Telephone: 0131 228 8484

CHILDSPLAY at 112 Tooting High Street, London SW17 ORR stock a range of toys, board games, books and cassettes. Telephone: 0181 672 6470

COMMUNITY INSIGHT carry a large range of books focusing on child development and equal opportunities issues for adults, and their children's books compliment anti-racist practice. Pembroke Centre, Cheney Manor, Swindon SN2 2PQ. Telephone: 01793 512612

COMMISSION FOR RACIAL EQUALITY CRE 10-12 Allington Street, London SW1E 5EH Telephone: 0171 828 7022

DAYCARE TRUST Wild Court, London WC2B 4AU. Telephone: 0171 405 5617/8

EARLY CHILDHOOD UNIT National Children's Bureau, 8 Wakley Street, London EC1V 7QE. Telephone: 0171 843 6000. The National Children's Bureau have published a useful resource With Equal Concern (1995).

EARLY YEARS TRAINERS ANTI-RACIST NETWORK (EYTARN) P O Box 1870, London N12 8JQ. Telephone: 0181 446 7056 Membership and orders to P O Box 28, Wallasey L45 9NP

EBONY EYES RAG DOLLS are black 'cabbage-patch' type dolls and hand puppets. Available from 10 Searson House, London SE17 3AY. Telephone: 0171 735 2887

EDU-PLAY has resources for play/therapy, learning difficulties and early learning at Vulcan Business Centre, Units H and I, Vulcan Road, Leicester LE5 3EB. Telephone: 0116 262 5827

EMANI PUBLICATIONS produces the *Black Like Me* series of workbooks by Jocelyn Maxime. From Suites 41-43 Melville Court, Croft Street, London SE8 5DR. Telephone: 0171 394 9024

EQUALITY LEARNING CENTRE, a Save the Children project which aims to build on the work developed by Building Blocks. 356 Holloway Road, London N7 6PA. Telephone: 0171 700 8127

GALT EDUCATIONAL have an extensive range of play equipment, Brookfield Road, Cheadle, Cheshire SK8 2PN. Telephone: 0161 428 8511

HANDPRINT publishes much-needed material on the contribution of Black women and men to human progress. Catalogue from 9 Key Hill Drive, Birmingham B18 5NY. Telephone: 0121 551 7524

HEIGHTS CULTURE SHOP specialises in literature and handicrafts from Africa, India and the Caribbean. Bowes, Lion House, St George's Way, Stevenage SG1 1XY. Telephone: 01438 722 435

INVICTA BOOK SERVICE specialises in non-racist and non-sexist publications at 162 Coppice Street, Oldham OL8 4BJ. Telephone: 0161 620 63981

KIDS CLUB NETWORK Bellerive House, 3 Muirfield Crescent, London E14 9SZ. Telephone: 0171 512 2112

KNOCK ON WOOD supplies a comprehensive range of music – instruments, books and recordings at Granary Wharf, Leeds LS1 4BR. Telephone: 0113 2429 146

LETTERBOX LIBRARY is the only book club specialising in non-sexist and multicultural books for children. Unit 2D Second Floor, Leroy House, 436 Essex Road, London N1 3QP. Telephone: 0171 226 1633. *Books of Black Heroes* Volumes 1 and 2 are available from Letterbox.

LILLIAN REEVES is once again making her appealing and cuddly rag dolls with a variety of physical features, skin colours and hair styles. Telephone: 0171 221 2630

MINORITY RIGHTS GROUP 29 Craven Street, London WC2N 5NT

MULTICULTURAL INFORMATION PACK An Information pack for use in residential homes and other childcare settings, including information on hair care, diet, health, cultural celebrations. For viewing or loan. Telephone: 01865 815005

NATIONAL CHILDMINDING ASSOCIATION 8 Masons Hill, Bromley BR2 9EY. Telephone: 0191 464 6164

NATIONAL COUNCIL OF VOLUNTARY CHILD CARE ORGANISATIONS 80 White Lion Street, London N1 9PF

NATIONAL EARLY YEARS NETWORK (formerly VOLCUF) 77 Holloway Road, London N7 Telephone: 0171 607 9573

NES ARNOLD distribute a wide range of play equipment. Ludlow Hill Road, West Bridgeford, Nottingham NG2 6HD. Telephone: 0115 945 2201

NEWS FROM NOWHERE feminist bookshop at 112 Bold Street, Liverpool L1.

POSITIVE IMAGES collection of toys etc representing small manufacturers at 5 Wood Cliff Drive, Chiselhurst, Kent BR7 5NT.

PRE SCHOOL EDUCATION RESOURCE CENTRE supplies a comprehensive range of play materials at 2-4 Roscoe Street, Liverpool L1 2SX. Telephone: 0151 708 7698

PRE-SCHOOL LEARNING ALLIANCE (formerly PPA) 61 King's Cross Road, London WC1X 9LL. Telephone: 0171 833 0991

RADDLE BOOKS 70 Berners Street, Leicester LE2 OAF specialise in African, Caribbean and African-American books, arts, crafts and records. Telephone: 0116 2624875

REDI HOBBIES produce well made wooden puzzles at Hawthorne Cottages, 153 Redehall Road, Horley RH6 9RJ. Telephone: 01342 717538

ROY YATES BOOKS specialises in dual-language books for children. Smallfields Cottage, Cox Green, Horsham RH12 3DE. Telephone: 01403 822299

SICKLE CELL SOCIETY 54 Station Road, London NW10 7UA. Telephone: 0181 961 7795

SEED PUBLICATIONS publishes books, greeting cards and posters – mail order P O Box 852, London W11 4RY. Telephone: 0171 603 8523

SOMA BOOKS stocks a wide range of books on South Asia, Africa and the Caribbean and specialise in dual text books for children. 38 Kennington Lane, London SE11 4LS. Telephone: 0171 735 2101

SOURCE BOOKS specialises in Black literature and educational materials at 3 Myrtle Parade, Liverpool 7.

STEP BY STEP is a mail order company specialising in products for the under-fives. 34 Lavenham Road, Beeches Trading Estate, Bristol BS17 5QX. Telephone: 01454 3202 200

SUPPORT AND TRAINING AGAINST RACISM FOR UNDER FIVES WORKERS AND PARENTS (STAR) 7 Barton Buildings, Bath BA1 2JR

TAMARIND LIMITED P O Box 296 Camberley, Surrey GU15 1QW produces books, puzzles and sequence cards which seek to challenge ethnic and gender stereotyping. Telephone: 01279 683 979 for catalogue.

TRAINING PACK The Changing Face of Britain – Different Cultures of Britain's major ethnic communities (two books and videos plus Information Sheet for training) £63.50. Telephone: 01374 420025

TRENTHAM BOOKS publishes a wide and interesting range of publications with a section on Education including a number on the Early Years. Westview House, 734 London Road, Stoke-on-Trent. Telephone: 01782 745567 or fax 01782-745553 for free catalogue. Their *Spanner in the Works* (1991) has some excellent ideas for work with children.

UNICEF Unit 1, Rignals Lane, Chelmsford, Essex CM2 8TU produce a catalogue with their current list of publications such as One World and The Equaliser II , which have been referred to in this manual.

UNITED KINGDON THALASSAEMIA SOCIETY 107 Nightingale Lane, London N8 7QY. Telephone: 0181 348 0437

WOODCRAFT FOLK 13 Ritherdon Road, London SW17 8QE

WORKING FOR CHILDCARE 77 Holloway Road, London N7 8JZ. Telephone: 0171 700 0281

WORKING GROUP AGAINST RACISM IN CHILDREN'S RESOURCES (WGARCR) 460 Wandsworth Road, London SW8 3LX. Telephone: 0171 627 4594

WORLDWISE retails a range of books, dolls, puppets, posters, card and board games to promote anti-racist multicultural practice. The organiser is happy to exhibit these materials at events. 60 Holgate Road, York YO2 4AB. Telephone: 01904 647340

ZADI is an Afro-Caribbean teenage vinyl doll produced by Star Apple Blossoms Limited, 13 Inman Road, London SW18 3BB

ZUMA ART SERVICES are large importers of posters, prints. They are at The Howitt Building, London Business Centre, London Boulevard, Nottingham NG7 2BD. Tel: 0115 952 1961

BIBLIOGRAPHY

Argyle, M., *Social Interaction*, Metheun, 1969.

Banks, N., Some considerations of racial identification and self esteem when working with mixed ethnicity children and their mothers as social services clients. *Social Services Research No. 3,* Birmingham University.

Barton, in Banks, N., Some considerations of racial identification and self esteem when working with mixed ethnicity children and their mothers as social services clients. *Social Services Research No. 3*, Birmingham University, 1959.

Benson, S., in Wilson, A., *Mixed Race Children; a study of identity*, Allen and Unwin, 1987.

Billig, M., Condor, S., Edwards, D., Gane, M., Middleton, D. and Radley, A., *Ideological Dilemmas: a social psychology of everyday thinking*, Sage, London, 1988, pp. 106-9.

Billig et al. in Troyna, B., and Carrington, B., *Education, Racism and Reform*, Routledge, London, 1990.

Brown, C., *Black and White Britain: the third PSI survey,* Heinemann/Gower, 1984.

Brown, C., Same Difference: The persistence of racial disadvantage in the British employment market in Braham, P., Rattansi, A., Skellington, R., (eds), *Racism and Antiracism*, Sage Publications, 1992.

Cooley, C.H., *Human Nature and the Social Order*, Schreiber, New York, 1902.

Cross, W., A two factor theory of black identity: implications for the study of identity development in minority children, J Phinney and J Rotherham – *Children's Ethnic Socialisation*, 1987.

Derman-Sparks, L., *Anti Bias Curriculum – Tools for Empowering Young Children*, NAEYC, 1989 (available from Community Insight – see page 58).

Dover, C., in Wilson, A., *Mixed Race Children; a study of identity*, Allen and Unwin, 1987.

Erikson, E., *Identity and the life cycle*, Norton, New York, 1980. Childhood and Society, 1963.

EYTARN, *The Best of Both Worlds – Celebrating Mixed Parentage*, Conference report, 1995.

Garret, H., lecture notes from Module on Equity Issues, Postgraduate Diploma/MA in Equity and Change in the Public Services, Department of Community Studies, University of Reading, 1996.

Glamour magazine, 1955 in Wilson, A., *Mixed Race Children; a study of identity*, Allen and Unwin, 1987.

Goldstein, Beverley Prevatt, *Image and Identity: Mixed Parentage Conference Report*, EYTARN, 1995.

Hendriks, J.H., and Figueroa J., *Black in White – The Caribbean Child in the UK*, Pitman Books.

Hill, (1965) in Banks, N., Some considerations of racial identification and self esteem when working with mixed ethnicity children and their mothers as social services clients. *Social Services Research No. 3*, Birmingham University.

Hicks, D., and Steiner, M., (eds) *Making Global Connections, A World Studies Workbook*, Oliver and Boyd, 1989.

Hume, D., lecture notes from Module on Equity Issues, Postgraduate Diploma/MA in Equity and Change in the Public Services, Department of Community Studies, University of Reading, 1996.

Jones, E.E., and Gerard, H.B., *Foundations of Social Psychology*, Wiley, 1967.

Kelly, E. and Cohn, T., *Racism in Schools; new research evidence*, Trentham Books, 1988.

Long, E., in Wilson, A., *Mixed Race Children; a study of identity*, Allen and Unwin, 1987.

McFarlane, C., *Behind the Scenes*, Development Education Centre, Birmingham, 1988.

Mandela, N., *Long Walk to Freedom*, Longsight Press, 1994.

Mason, D., *Race and Ethnicity in Modern Britain*, Oxford University Press, 1995.

Maxime, J.E., Some psychological models of black self concept, in Ahmed, S., Cheetham, J., and Small, J., (eds), *Social Work with Black children and their families*, Batsford, 1986.

Maxime, J.E., The importance of racial identity for the psychological well-being of Black children, ACPP Vol.15, No. 4, 1993.

Maxime, J.E., in Varma, V., (ed), *How and why children hate: a study of conscious and unconscious sources*, Jessica Kingsley, 1993.

Mead, G.H., *Mind, Self and Society*, University of Chicago Press, 1934.

Milner,D., *Children and Race Ten Years On*, Ward Lock, 1983.

National Children's Bureau, *Ensuring Standards*, 1991.

National Youth Agency, *A race and Culture Activity Pack*, Leicester (te. 0116 285 6789; price £8.50)

Nobles, W., Psychological research and the black self concept: a critical review , *Journal of Social Issues*, 1973.

Richards, W., (paper) Working with mixed race young people, Community and Youth Studies, Westhill College, Birmingham.

Rose, Lewontin and Kamin, lecture notes from Module on Equity Issues, Postgraduate Diploma/MA in Equity and Change in the Public Services, Department of Community Studies, University of Reading, 1996.

Ryburn, M., *Identity and openness: Adoption in the 1990s*, Leamington Press, 1992.

Siraj-Blatchford, I., *The Early Years; laying the foundations for racial equality* Trentham Books, 1994.

Terman, L., lecture notes from Module on Equity Issues, Postgraduate Diploma/MA in Equity and Change in the Public Services, Department of Community Studies, University of Reading, 1996.

Tizard, B., and Phoenix, A., Black Identity and Transracial Adoption, *New Community 15* (3) 427-437, April 1989.

Troyna B., and Carrington, B., *Education, Racism and Reform*, Routledge, 1990.

UNICEF (UK) and Save the Children, Book 2, *It's Our Right*, 1990.

Wilson, A., *Mixed Race Children; a study of identity*, Allen and Unwin, 1987.